Silas Weir Mitchell

Mr. Kris Kringl

a Christmas tale

Silas Weir Mitchell

Mr. Kris Kringl
a Christmas tale

ISBN/EAN: 9783741135415

Manufactured in Europe, USA, Canada, Australia, Japa

Cover: Foto ©Thomas Meinert / pixelio.de

Manufactured and distributed by brebook publishing software
(www.brebook.com)

Silas Weir Mitchell

Mr. Kris Kringl

MR. KRIS KRINGLE.

A

Christmas Tale.

BY

S. WEIR MITCHELL, M. D., LL. D., HARVARD.

FIFTH THOUSAND.

PHILADELPHIA :
GEORGE W. JACOBS & CO.,
103 South 15th Street,
1894.

The following little Christmas story was written, and is published for the benefit of the Home of the Merciful Saviour for Crippled Children, Philadelphia.

S. WEIR MITCHELL.

MR. KRIS KRINGLE.

IT was Christmas Eve. The snow had clad the rolling hills in white, as if in preparation for the sacred morrow. The winds, boisterous all day long, at fall of night ceased to roar amidst the naked forest, and now, the silent industry of the falling flakes made of pine and spruce tall white tents. At last, as the darkness grew, a deepening stillness came on hill and valley, and all nature seemed to wait expectant of the coming of the Christmas time.

5

Above the broad river a long, gray stone house lay quiet; its vine and roof heavy with the softly-falling snow, and showing no sign of light or life except in a feeble, red glow through the Venetian blinds of the many windows of one large room. Within, a huge fire of mighty logs lit up with distinctness only the middle space, and fell with variable illumination on a silent group about the hearth.

On one side a mother sat with her cheek upon her hand, her elbow on the table, gazing steadily into the fire; on the other side were two children, a girl and a boy; he on a cushion, she in a low chair. Some half-felt sadness repressed for these little ones the usual gay Christmas humor of the hopeful hour, commonly so full for them of that anticipative joy to which life brings shadowy sadness as the years run on.

Now and then the boy looked across the room, pleased when the leaping flames sent flaring over floor and wall long shadows from the tall brass andirons or claw-footed chair and table. Sometimes he glanced shyly at the mother, but getting no answering smile kept silence. Once or twice the girl whispered a word to him, as the logs fell and a sheet of flame from the hickory and the quick-burning birch set free the stored-up sunshine of many a summer day. A moment later, the girl caught the boy's arm.

"Oh! hear the ice, Hugh," she cried, for mysterious noises came up from the river and died away.

"Yes, it is the ice, dear," said the mother.

"I like to hear it." As she spoke she struck a match and lit two candles which stood on the table beside her.

For a few minutes as she stood her gaze wandered along the walls over the portraits of men and women once famous in Colonial days. The great china bowls, set high for safety on top of the book-cases, tankards, and tall candelabra troubled her with memories of more prosperous times. Whatever emotions these relics of departed pride and joy excited, they left neither on brow nor on cheek the unrelenting signals of life's disasters. A glance distinctly tender and distinctly proud made sweet her face for a moment as she turned to look upon the children.

The little fellow on the cushion at her feet looked up.

"Mamma, we do want to know why Christ-mas comes only once a year?"

"Hush, dear, I cannot talk to you now; not to-night; not at all, to-night."

"But was not Christ always born?" he persisted.

"Yes, yes," she replied. "But I cannot talk to you now. Be quiet a little while. I have something to do," and so saying, she drew to her side a basket of old letters.

The children remained silent, or made little signs to one another as they watched the fire. Meanwhile the mother considered the papers, now with a gleam of anger in her eyes, as she read, and now with a momentary blur of tear-dimmed vision. Most of the letters she threw at once on the fire. They writhed a moment like living creatures, and of a sudden blazed out as if tormented into sudden confession of the passions of years gone by; then they fell away to black unmemoried things, curling crumpled in the heat.

The children saw them burn with simple interest in each new conflagration. Something in the mother's ways quieted them, and they became intuitively conscious of sadness in the hour and the task. At last the boy grew uneasy at the long repose of tongue.

"O Alice! see the red sparks going about," he said, looking at the wandering points of light in the blackening scrolls of shrivelled paper.

"Nurse says those are people going to church," said his sister, authoritatively.

Her mother looked up, smiling. "Ah,

that is what they used to tell me when I was little."

" 'They're fire-flies," said the boy, " like in a vewy dark night." Now and then his r's troubled him a little, and conscious of his difficulty, he spoke at times with oddly serious deliberation.

"You really must be quiet," said the mother. "Now, do keep still, or you will have to go to bed," and so saying she turned anew to the basket.

Presently the girl exclaimed, "Why do you burn the letters?" She had some of her mother's persistency, and was not readily controlled. This time the mother made no reply. A sharp spasm of pain went over her features. Looking into the fire, as if altogether unconscious of the quick spies at her side, she said aloud, "Oh! I can no more! Let them wait. What a fool I was. What a fool!" and abruptly pushed the basket aside.

The little fellow leaped up and cast his arms about her while his long, yellow hair fell on her neck and shoulder. "O Mamma!" he cried, "don't read any more. Let *me* burn them. I hate them to hurt you."

She smiled on him through tears—rare things for her. "Every one must bear his own troubles, Hugh. You couldn't help me. You couldn't know, dear, what to burn."

"But I know," said the girl, decisively. I know. I had a letter once; but Hugh never had a letter. I wish Kris Kringle would take them away this very, very night; and lessons, too, I do. What will he bring us for Christmas, mamma? I know what. I want "—

"A Kris Kringle to take away troubles would suit me well, Alice; I could hang up a big stocking."

"And I know what I want," said the boy. "Nurse says Kris has no money this Christmas. I don't care." But the great blue eyes filled as he spoke.

The mother rose. "There will be no presents this year, Hugh. Only—only more love from me, from one another; and you must be brave and help me, because you know this is not the worst of it. We are to go away next week, and must live in the town. You see, dears, it can't be helped."

"Yes," said Hugh, thoughtfully, "it can't be helped, Alice."

"I don't want to go," said the girl.

"Hush," said Hugh.

"And I do want a doll."

"I told you to be quiet, Alice," returned the mother, a rising note of anger in her voice. In fact, she was close upon a burst of tears, but the emotions are all near of kin and linked in mystery of relationship. Pity and love for the moment became unreasoning wrath. "You are disobedient," she continued.

"O mamma! we are vewy sorry," said the lad, who had been the less offending culprit.

"Well, well. No matter. It is bed-time, children. Now to bed, and no more nonsense. I can't have it, I can't bear it."

The children rose submissively, and, kiss-

ing her, were just leaving the room, when
she said : " Oh! but we must not lose our
manners. You forget."

The girl, pausing near the doorway, dropped
a courtesy.

" That wasn't very well done, Alice. Ah!
that was better."

The little fellow made a bow quite worthy
of the days of minuet and hoop, and then,
running back, kissed the tall mother with a
certain passionate tenderness, saying, softly,
" Now, don't you cry when we are gone, dear,
dear mamma," and then, in a whisper, " I will
pway God not to let you cwy," and so fled
away, leaving her still perilously close to tears.
Very soon, up-stairs, the old nurse, troubled by the children's disappointment, was
assuring them with eager mendacity that

Kris would be certain to make his usual visit, while down-stairs the mother walked slowly to and fro. She had that miserable gift, an unfailing memory of anniversaries, and now, despite herself, the long years rolled back upon her, so that under the sad power of their recurrent memories she seemed a helpless prey.

While the children were yet too young to recognize their loss the great calamity of her life had come. Then by degrees the wreck of her fortune had gone to pieces, and now at last the home of her own people, deeply mortgaged, was about to pass from her forever. Much that was humbling had fallen to her in life, but nothing as sore as this final disaster. At length she rose, took a lighted candle from the table, and walked

AND OPENED THE CASE OF A MINIATURE, SLOWLY AND WITH
DELIBERATE CARE.

Page 17.

slowly around the great library room. The
sombre bindings of the books her childhood
knew called back dim recollections. The
great china bowls, the tall silver tankards,
the shining sconces, and above, all the Stuart
portraits or the Copleys of the men who shone
in Colonial days and helped to make a more
than imperial nation, each and all disturbed
her as she gazed. At last, she returned to the
fireside, sat down and began anew her un-
finished task. With hasty hands she tumbled over the letters, and at length came
upon a package tied with a faded ribbon;
one of those thin orange-colored silk bands
with which cigars are tied in bundles. She
threw it aside with a quick movement of
disdain, and opened the case of a miniature,
slowly, and with deliberate care. A letter

2

fell on to her lap as she bent over the portrait of a young man. The day, the time, the need to dispose of accumulated letters, had brought her to this which she meant to be a final settlement of one of life's grim accounts. For awhile, she steadily regarded the relics of happier hours. Then, throwing herself back in her chair, she cried aloud, " How long I hoped ; how hopeless was my hope, and he said, he said, I was cruel and hard. That I loved him no more. Oh! that was a lie! a bitter lie! But a sot, a sot, and my children to grow up and see what I saw, and learn to bear what I have borne. No! no! a thousand times no! I chose between two duties, and I was right. I was the man of the two, and I sent him away—forever. He said,—yes, I was right,

but, my God! how cruel is life! I would
never have gone, never! never! There!"
she exclaimed, and threw back the miniature
into the basket, closing it with violence, as
she did so, as one may shut an unpleasant
book read and done with.

For a moment, and with firmer face, she
considered the letter, reading scraps of it
aloud, as if testing her resolution to make an
end of it all. "Hard, was I? Yes. Would I
had been sooner hard. My children would have
been better off. 'I went because you bid me.'
Yes I did. Will he ever know what that cost
me? 'I shall never come again until you bid
me come.' Not in this world then?" she cried.
"O Hugh! Hugh!" And in a passion of tears
that told of a too great trial, still resolute
despite her partial defeat, she tore the letter

and cast it on the fire. "There!" she cried, "would to God I loved him less." And then, with strange firmness, she took up a book, and sternly set herself to comprehend what she read.

The hours went by and at last she rose wearily, put out one candle, raked ashes over the embers, and taking the other light, went slowly up to bed. She paused a moment at the nursery door where she heard voices. "What! awake still?"

"We was only talking about Khwis," said the small boy. "We won't any more, will we, Alice? She thinks he won't come, but I think he will come because we are both so good all to-day."

"No, no, he will not come this Christmas, my darlings. Go to sleep. Go to sleep," and with too full a heart she turned away.

But the usual tranquil slumber of childhood was not theirs. The immense fact that they were soon to leave their home troubled the imaginative little man. Then, too, a great wind began to sweep over the hills and to shake the snow-laden pines. On its way, it carried anew from the ice of the river wild sounds of disturbance and at last, in the mid hours of night, an avalanche of snow slid from the roof. Hugh sat up; he realized well enough what had happened. But presently the quick ear of childhood was aware of other, and less familiar sounds. Was it Kris Kringle? Oh! if he could only see him once! He touched the sister asleep in her bed near by, and at last shook her gently.

"What is it, Hugh?" she said.

"I hear Khwis. I know it is Khwis!"

"O Hugh! I hear too, but it might be a robber."

"No, nevah on Chwistmas Eve. It couldn't be a wobber. It is Khwis. I mean to go and see. I hear him outside. You know, Alice, there is nevah, nevah any wickedness on Chwistmas Eve."

"But if it is a robber he might take you away."

"Oh! wobbers steal girls, but they nevah, nevah steal boys, and you needn't go."

"But are you sure? Oh! do listen," she added. Both heard the creaking noise of footsteeps in the dry snow.

"I will look—I must look," cried Hugh, slipping from his bed. In a moment he had raised the sash and was looking out

"Mr. Khwis Kwingle, Are You There? Or Is' You A Wobber?"

into the night. The sounds he had heard
ceased. He could see no one. " He has
gone, Alice." Then he cried, " Mr. Khwis
Kwingle, are you there? or is you a wobber?" As he spoke a cloaked man came
from behind a great pine and stood amid
the thickly-fallen flakes.

" Why, that is Hugh," he said. " Hugh!"

" He does know my name," whispered the
lad to the small counsellor now at his
side.

" And, of course, I am Kris Kringle. And
I have a bag full of presents. But come
softly down and let me in, and don't make
a noise or away I go; and bring Alice."

The girl was still in doubt, but her desire
for the promised gifts was strong, and in
the very blood of the boy was the spirit

of daring adventure. There was a moment of whispered indecision, resulting in two bits of conclusive wisdom.

Said Alice, "If we go together, Hugh, and he takes one, the other can squeal. Oh! very loud like a bear—a *big* bear."

"And," said Hugh, "I will get my gweat gwandpapa's sword." And with this he got upon a chair and by the failing light of the nursery fire carefully took down from over the chimney the dress rapier which had figured at peaceful levees of other days. "Now," he said, "if you are afwaid I will go all alone myself."

"I am dreadfully afraid," said she, "but I will go, too." So she hastily slipped on a little white wrapper and he his well-worn brown velvet knickerbocker trousers. Neither

had ever known a being they had reason to
fear, and so, with beating hearts, but brave
enough, they stole quietly out in their sweet
innocence and hand in hand went down the
dark staircase, still hearing faint noises as
they felt their way. They crossed the great
warm library and entered the hall, where,
with much effort, they unlocked the door
and lifted the old-fashioned bar which guarded
it. The cold air swept in, and before them
was a tall man in a cloak half white with
snow. He said at once, "Oh! Hugh! Alice!
Pleasant Christmas to you. Let us get in
out of the cold; but carefully—carefully, no
sound!" As he spoke he shut the door
behind him. "Come," he said, and seeming
to know the way, went before them into the
library.

"Oh! I'm so frightened," said Alice to Hugh in a whisper. "I wish I was in bed."

Not so the boy. The man pushed away the ashes from the smouldering logs, and took from the wood basket a quantity of birch bark and great cones of the pine. As he cast them on the quick embers a fierce red blaze went up, and the room was all alight. And now he turned quickly, for Hugh, of a mind to settle the matter, was standing on guard between him and the door to the stairway, which they had left open when they came down. The man smiled as he saw the lad push his sister back and come a step or two forward. He made a pretty picture in his white shirt, brown knee-breeches, and little bare legs, the yellow

HE MADE A PRETTY PICTURE—ALERT AND QUITE FEARLESS.

Page 26.

locks about his shoulders, the rapier in his hand, alert and quite fearless.

"My sister thinks perhaps you are a wobber, sir; but I think you are Mr. Khwis Kwingle."

"Yes, I am Kris Kringle to-night, and you see I know your names—Alice, Hugh." His cloak fell from him, and he stood smiling, a handsome Chris. "Do not be afraid. Be sure I love little children. Come, let us talk a bit."

"It's all wite, Alice," said the boy. "I said he wasn't a wobber."

And they went hand in hand toward the fire, now a brilliant blaze. The man leaned heavily upon a chair back, his lips moving, a great stir of emotion shaking him as he gazed on the little ones. But he said again, quickly:

"Yes, yes, I'm Kris Kringle," and then, with much amusement, "and what do you mean to do with your sword, my little man?"

"It was to kill the wobber, sir; but you mustn't be afraid, because you're not a wobber."

"And he really won't hurt you," added Alice.

"Good gracious!" exclaimed Kris, smiling, "you're a gallant little gentleman. And you have been—are you always a good boy to—your mother?"

"I has been a vewy good boy." Then his conscience entered a protest, and he added : "for two whole days. I'll go and ask mamma to come and tell you."

"No, no," said Kris. "It is only chil-

dren can see me. Old folks couldn't see
me."

"My mother is vewy young."

"Oh! but not like a child; not like you."

"Please, sir, to let us see the presents,"
said Alice, much at her ease. For now he
pushed a great chair to the fire, and seated
them both in it, saying: "Ah! the poor
little cold toes." Then he carefully closed
the door they had left open, and said, smiling as he sat down opposite them: "I have
come far—very far—to see you."

"Has you come far to-night?" said the
little host, with rising courage.

"No, not far to-night." Then he paused.
"Is—is your mother—well?"

"Yes," said Hugh, "she is vewy well, and
we are much obliged."

"May we soon see the presents?" said Alice. "They did say you would not come to-night because we are poor now."

"And," added Hugh, "my pony is sold to a man, and his tail is vewy long, and he loves sugar—the pony, I mean; and mamma says we must go away and live in the town."

"Yes, yes," said Kris. "I know."

"He knows," said Hugh.

"Oh! they know everything in fairyland," said Alice.

"Was you evah in faywyland, sir?" asked Hugh.

"Yes."

"Where 'bouts is it, sir, and please how is it bounded on the north? And what are the pwincipal wivers? We might look for it on the map."

"It is in the Black Hills."

"Oh! the Black Hills," said Alice. "I know."

"Yes, but you're not sleepy? Not a bit sleepy?"

"No, no."

"Then before the pretty things hop out of my bag let me tell you a story," and he smiled at his desire to lengthen a delicious hour.

"I would like that."

"And I hope it won't be very, very long," said Alice, on more sordid things intent.

"That's the way with girls, Mr. Kwingle; they can't wait."

"Ah, well, well. Once on a time there was a bad boy, and he was very naughty, and no one loved him because he spent love like money till it was all gone. When he found he had no more love given him, he went away, and away, to a far country."

"Like the man in the Bible," said Hugh, promptly. "The—the—what's his name, Alice?"

"The prodigal son," said Kris, "you mean—"

"Yes, sir. The pwodigal son."

"Yes, like the prodigal son."

"Well, at last he came to the Black Hills, and there he lived with other rough men."

"But you did say he was a boy," said Alice, accurately critical.

"He was gwowed up, Alice. Don't you int— inter—"

"Interrupt, you goosey," said Alice.

"One Christmas Eve these men fell to talking of their homes, and made up their minds to have a good dinner. But Hugh—"

"Oh!" exclaimed the lad, "Hugh!"

Mr. Chris nodded and continued. "But Hugh felt very weak because he was just getting well of a fever, yet they persuaded him to come to table with the rest. One man, a German, stood up and said, 'This is the eve of Christmas. I will say our grace what we say at home.' One man laughed, but the others were still. Then the German said,

'Come, Lord Christ, and be our guest,
Take with us what Thou hast blest.'

When Hugh heard the words the German said he began to think of home and of many Christmas eves, and because he felt a

3

strangeness in his head, he said, 'I'm not
well; I will go into the air.' As he moved,
he saw before him a man in the doorway.
The face of the man was sad, and his gar-
ment was white as snow. He said, 'Follow
me.' But no others, except Hugh, saw or
heard. Now, when Hugh went outside, the
man he had seen was gone; but being still
confused, Hugh went over the hard snow and
among trees, not knowing what he did; and
at last after wandering a long time he came
to a steep hillside. Here he slipped and
rolling down fell over a high place. Down,
down, down he fell, and he fell."

"Oh! make him stop," cried little Hugh.

"He fell on to a deep bed of soft snow
and was not hurt, but soon got up, and
thought he was buried in a white tomb.

But soon he understood, and his head grew clearer, and he beat the snow away and got out. Then, first he said a prayer, and that was the only prayer he had said in a long time."

"Oh my!" cried little Hugh. "I did think people could nevah sleep unless they say their prayers. That's what nurse says. Doesn't she, Alice?"

And just here Kris had to wipe his eyes, but he took the little fellow's hand in his and went on.

"Soon he found shelter under a cliff, where no snow was, and with his flint and steel struck a light, and made with sticks and logs a big fire. After this he felt warm and better all over and fell asleep. When he woke up it was early morning, and looking about, he saw in the rock little yellow streaks and small lumps, and then he knew he had found a great mine of gold no man had ever seen before. By and by he got out of the valley and found his companions, and in the spring he went to his mine, which, because he had found it, was all his own, and he got people to work there and dig out the gold. After that he was no longer poor, but very, very rich."

"And was he good then?" said Hugh.

"And did he go home," said Alice, "and buy things?"

"Yes, he went. One day he went home and at night saw his house and little children, and—but he will not stay, because there is no love waiting in his house, and all the money in the world is no good unless there is some love too. You see, dear, a house is just a house of brick and mortar, but when it is full of love, then it is a home."

"I like that man," said Hugh. "Tell me more."

"But first," said Alice, "oh! we do want to see all our presents."

"Ah, well. That is all, I think; and the presents. Now for the presents." Then he opened a bag and took out first a string of great pearls, and said, as he hung them around Alice's neck, "There, these the oysters made for you years ago under the deep blue sea. They are for a wedding gift from Chris. They are too fine for a little maid. No Queen has prettier pearls. But when you are married and some one you love vexes you or is unkind, look at these pearls, and forgive, oh! a hundred times over; twice, thrice, for every pearl, because Kris said it. You won't understand now, but some day you will."

"Yes, sir," said Alice, puzzled, and playing with the pearls.

Said Hugh, "You said, Mr. Khwis, that the oysters make pearls. Why do the oysters make pearls?"

"I will tell you," replied Kris. "If a bit of something rough or sharp gets inside the oyster's house, and it can't be got rid of, the oyster begins to make a pearl of it, and covers it over and over until the rough, rude thing is one of these beautiful pearls."

"I see," said Hugh.

"That is a little fairy tale I made for myself; I often make stories for myself."

"That must be very nice, Mr. Khwis. How nice it must be for your little children every night when you tell them stories."

"Yes—yes"—and here Kris had to wipe his eyes with his handkerchief.

"Isn't that a doll?" said Alice, looking at the bag.

"Yes; a doll from Japan."

"Oh!" exclaimed Alice.

"And boxes of sugar-plums for Christmas," he added. "And, Hugh, here are skates for you and this bundle of books."

"Thank you, sir."

"And these—and these for my—for Alice," and Kris drew forth a half-dozen delicate Eastern scarves and cast them, laughing, around the girl's neck as she stood delighted.

"And now I want to trust you. This is
for—for your mother; only an envelope from
Kris to her. Inside is a fairy paper, and
whenever she pleases it will turn to gold—
oh! much gold, and she will be able then
to keep her old home and you need never
go away, and the pony will stay."

"Oh! that will be nice. We do sank
you, sir; don't we, Alice?"

"Yes. But now I must go. Kiss me.
You *will* kiss me?" He seemed to doubt it.

"Oh! yes," they cried, and cast their little
arms about him while he held them in a
long embrace, loath to let them go.

"O Alice!" said Hugh, "Mr. Khwis is
cwying. What's the matter, Mr. Khwis?"

"Nothing," he said. "Once I had two
little children, and you see you look like

them, and—and I have not seen them this
long while."

Alice silently reflected on the amount of
presents which Kris's children must have,
but Hugh said:

"We are bofe wewy sorry for you, Mr.
Khwis."

"Thank you," he returned, "I shall re-
member that, and now be still a little, I
must write to your mother, and you must
give her my letter after she has my present."

"Yes," said Alice, "we will."

Then Kris lit a candle and took paper
and pen from the table, and as they sat
quietly waiting, full of the marvel of this
famous adventure, he wrote busily, now and
then pausing to smile on them, until he
closed and gave the letter to the boy.

"Be careful of these things," he said, "for now I must go."

"And will you nevah, nevah come back?"

"My God!" cried the man. "Never—perhaps never. Don't forget me, Alice, Hugh." And this time he kissed them again and went by and opened the door to the stairway.

"We thank you ever so much," said Hugh, and standing aside he waited for Alice to pass, having in his child-like ways something of the grave courtesy of the ancestors who looked down on him from the walls. Alice courtesied and the small cavalier, still with the old rapier in hand, bowed low. Kris stood at the door and listened to the patter of little feet upon the stair; then he closed it with noiseless care. In a few

minutes he had put out the candles, re-
sumed his cloak, and left the house. The
snow no longer fell. The waning night was
clearer, and to eastward a faint rosy gleam
foretold the coming of the sun of Christmas.
Kris glanced up at the long-windowed house
and turning went slowly down the garden
path.

Long before their usual hour of rising, the
children burst into the mother's room. "You
monkeys," she cried, smiling; "Merry Christmas to you! What is the matter?"

"Oh! he was here! he did come!" cried
Alice.

"Khwis was here," said Hugh. "I did
hear him in the night, and I told Alice it
was Khwis, and she said it was a wobber,
and I said it wasn't a wobber. And we

went to see, and it was a man. It was Khwis. He did say so."

"What! a man at night in the house! Are you crazy, children?"

"And Hugh took grandpapa's sword, and—"

" Gweat-gwanpapa's," said Hugh, with strict accuracy.

"You brave boy!" cried the woman, proudly. "And he stole nothing, and, oh! what a silly tale."

" But it *was* Khwis, mamma. He did give us things. I do tell you it was Khwis Kwingle."

"Oh! he gave us things for you, and for me, and for Hugh, and he gave me this," cried Alice, who had kept her hand behind her, and now threw the royal pearls on the bed amid a glory of Eastern scarves.

"Are we all bewitched?" cried the mother.

"Oh! and skates, and sugar-plums, and books, and a doll, and this for you. Oh! Khwis didn't forget nobody, mamma."

The mother seized and hastily opened the blank envelope which the boy gave her.

"What! what!" she cried, as she stared at the inclosure; "is this a jest?"

UNION TRUST CO., NEW YORK.

MADAME:—We have the honor to hold at your disposal the following registered United States bonds, in all amounting to ———."

The sum was a great fortune. The Trust Company was known to her, even its president's signature.

"What's the matter, mamma," cried Alice, amazed at the unusual look the calm mother's face wore as she arose from the bed, while the great pearls tumbled over and lay on the sunlit floor, and the fairy letter fell un-heeded. Her thoughts were away in the desert of her past life.

"And here, I forgot," said Hugh, " Mr. Khwis did write you a letter."

" Quick," she cried. " Give it to me." She opened it with fierce eagerness. Then she said, " Go away, leave me alone. Yes, yes, I will talk to you by and by. Go now." And she drove the astonished children from the room and sat down with her letter.

" DEAR ALICE:—Shall I say wife? I prom-ised to come no more until you asked me to come. I can stand it no longer. I came only meaning to see the dear home, and to send you and my dear children a remembrance, but I— You know the rest. If in those dark days the mother care and fear instinctively set aside what little love was left for me I do not now wonder. Was it well, or ill, what you did when you bid me go? In God's time I have learned to think it well. That hour is to me now like a blurred dream. To-day I can bless the anger and the sense of duty to our children which drove me forth—too debased a thing to realize my loss. I have won again my self-control, thank God! am a man once more. You have, have always had, my love. You have to-day again a dozen times the fortune I meanly squandered. I shall never touch it; it is yours and your children's. And now, Alice, is all love dead for me?

And is it Yes or No? And shall I be always to my little ones Kris, and to-night
a mysterious memory, or shall I be once
more

YOUR HUGH?

"A letter to the bank will find me."

As she read, the quick tears came aflood.
She turned to her desk and wrote in tremu-
lous haste, "Come, come at once," and ring-
ing for the maid, sent it off to the address
he gave. The next morning she dressed
with unusual care. At the sound of the
whistle of the train she went down to the
door. Presently, a strong, erect, eager man
came swiftly up the pathway. She was in
his arms a minute after, little Hugh ex-
claiming, "O Alice! Mr. Khwis is kissing
mamma!"

"O ALICE! MR. KHWIS IS KISSING MAMMA."

Page 48.